Greek Mythology

Enchanting Tales of the Ancient World

Isaiah Covington

©Copyright 2021 by Cascade Publishing

All rights reserved.

It is not legal to reproduce, duplicate, or transmit any part of this document in either electronic means or in printed format. Recording of this publication is strictly prohibited.

TABLE OF CONTENTS

Introduction 1

Chapter One: Prometheus and the Theft of Fire 2

Chapter Two: Pandora and Her Jar 9

Chapter Three: The Myth of Narcissus and Echo 16

Chapter Four: King Midas and his Golden Touch 26

Chapter Five: The Tale of Heracles and the 12 Labors 42

Conclusion 67

INTRODUCTION

From Zeus to Athena, Hades to Hermes, Greek mythology is teeming with gods, Titans, heroes, and tale after tale of adventure. Some may be familiar, and others may be new additions to your mental library. Explore the epics within and journey to the realm of Ancient Greece.

Time and bias have a way of altering text and even history as it ages. This book aims to bring a smoother impression, genuine emotions, and relatable characters to each myth that you read. So if you are returning to this genre hoping for something new or just starting your exploration, welcome and enjoy these retold myths!

CHAPTER ONE:

PROMETHEUS AND THE THEFT OF FIRE

At the beginning of time when the worlds light was dim and chaos reigned, the earth was ruled by Titans – formidable deities, and descendants of the primordial gods. A prodigious ten year war erupted between the gods of Olympus and the mighty Titans that walked the earth for supreme reign over the universe. A forward thinking titan named Prometheus, predicted the victory of the Olympians during the Titanomachy and decided to side with the gods. The world trembled with the clashes that came to pass, and the titans eventually fell to the triumphant gods. Prometheus along with his brother Epimetheus enthralled Zeus with their support and escaped imprisonment in the infernal depths of Tartarus unlike their brethren.

After the ten year clash had finally come to an end, the almighty Zeus ordered Prometheus and his younger brother Epimetheus to create and populate the Earth with the most diverse creatures and beasts. The brothers labored tirelessly on forming every creature from scratch, each of which was bestowed with a distinctive attribute. And so, the birds were gifted the ability to fly, the elephant was formed with great strength, and the fish were now equipped with the ability to swim the depths of the ocean. While all of the talents were distributed evenly among all beings, mankind was saved for last, as the Titans aspired to present them with a special trait. However, after molding man from clay, the brothers realized that all of the abilities had already been attributed to all of the other animals.

Prometheus was not content with this outcome. Man cowered in caves avoiding all forms of beasts, subsisting on fruits and berries. This was not Prometheus' intention for mankind. Feeling empathetic for man's weak and naked state, he journeyed to Mount Olympus to speak with Zeus about what he could do.

"Oh, powerful Zeus," Prometheus said, bowing as he entered the presence of the mighty god. "You have the victory you sought, and Olympus is safe once more, but the world of humanity is dark and cold."

"Allow me to visit the mortals and help them to build," Prometheus continued. "The threat to Olympus has been contained, and now there are other matters toward which I feel my attention would be better served."

Zeus stood in silence for several moments, staring straight at Prometheus. The Titan knew that Zeus had never been a man of many words, but this silence seemed to be heavy and thick. At the very least, he expected some back and forth from the god. Instead, the result was much different as expected.

"No, you will not, and that will be the end of it."

That was it. There was no further discussion, just a deadpan response, and then Zeus turned away. Prometheus was stunned and remained motionless. He wanted to argue back, to plead the case that without mankind, the world would be so much less of itself, but all he could do was stammer a few times and then leave. There was no room for negotiation in Zeus's world, and Prometheus knew that there was only one single path of action left to take…

In a serene, wooded area of Olympus there stood a workshop where the gods created the most brilliant of things. Prometheus knew that somewhere in this wondrous workshop, he might find some enchanted item or craft that would bring aid to humanity.

In the past, Prometheus had always displayed wisdom and forethought in any situation, as was proven by his shift to the side of the gods during the war of the titans. The actions he was taking now, however, seemed heavily driven by emotion. Blind to consequence and the deep rage of Zeus, the Titan broke his way into the workshop, and before long, he happened across the answer: fire. Such a power would transform the lives of the mortals below and grant them many opportunities.

Hasty as his decision was, Prometheus had the wherewithal to realize that he would never make it through Olympus and down the mountain if he carried this torch, alerting all to his location. Looking around the shop, he saw a large, hollow stalk from a cluster of fennel on a nearby table. Carefully he hid the fire within the stalk and watched as the light faded from view. The flame would not last forever, however, so he took a deep breath of determination and set off from the workshop.

If there had been a stag on the mountain that night, Prometheus would have slipped right by without causing the twitch of a tail. Silent as death, he moved from darkness to darkness until finally, he reached the decline that would lead down to where humanity languished. With each step, the depth of his actions brought a renewed hustle to his stride. He reached level ground in almost no time and began to see shadows moving in the distance. He had found humanity. With fire now at their disposal, mankind started to develop rapidly. Weapons and tools were created and man began to flourish. Prometheus was ecstatic, his creation was finally starting to materialize alike to his vision.

Zeus was many things—jealous, impetuous, and selfish—but when it came to Olympus, he was steadfast and always watching. When the sun rose, and Olympus began to wake, it didn't take Zeus very long to feel as though something was wrong within his royal paradise.

From the baths to the gleaming columns, he searched high and low in attempt to reveal what seemed out of place. Finally, he came to the workshop, and every sense within him was firing as though pointing him in the right direction. Slowly he treaded through the workshop, glancing around for a brief moment, until his eyes stopped on a dim corner of the structure. Eyes wide and jaw set, he began tossing everything aside, realizing now that something was definitely missing. After several minutes he stood panting amid the wreckage he had caused, the anger giving way to a violent roar.

"Where is my fire!?" Zeus bellowed.

The roar thundered from the top of Mount Olympus through every door and archway, sweeping past open windows, winding around trees until it found the ears it was meant for. Prometheus raised his head in alarm as he caught the echoes all around him. It was then that he knew. He was in trouble.

Prometheus, was not used to reacting in fear, yet there he was, rushing to leave the company of mankind. Somehow in the back of his mind, he knew that his haste would have no impact on the outcome, but still, he hurried. That all came to a halt when the ground began to shake, and tremendous gusts of wind knocked Prometheus off his feet. Dazed from the fall, he peered through the whirling dust to see the glowing, nearly incandescent figure of Zeus.

"Where is my fire?"

The words were simple, but the depth of the god's voice sent a shudder through every vein the Titan had. Prometheus noticed his hands shaking, and he tried to stammer out any words at all.

"M-my...I only...I-I–" Prometheus couldn't seem to complete a sentence, let alone a single word, but the fire from Zeus's eyes closed his mouth quickly enough. The mighty god didn't even care to speak again but instead looked around with a determined swiftness. Seeming to see through solid objects, he continued to move about the region until he came across the fennel stalk. With a snort of air through his nose like a stallion, Zeus threw aside the stalk and held the flame aloft with one hand and while the other pointed directly at Prometheus.

"You will regret what you have done Prometheus, for each passing day until the end of time!" Zeus's thunderous voice slammed into Prometheus's ears and left the world ringing around him. Then everything went a very painful black.

Salt, Prometheus thought, *Salt and birds. Why does it smell like–*

His eyes shot open, and what he saw stopped all the sounds from coming from his throat. Hot, angry tears began to stream down his face as he looked out on the crashing waves of the ocean. As he moved forward, his arms and legs would not respond as normal. He peered over to his wrists then ankles, and screamed as he struggled to break free from the chains binding him to a giant rock. He thrashed and strained until blood covered the restraints, but nothing budged, and he was left sobbing and exhausted in the scorching sun.

A shadow covered the Titan momentarily from the sun before a sudden shock of pain that was worse than anything he had ever experienced. Shooting and stabbing at the same time, he looked down, and to his absolute horror, he saw an eagle tearing at his side with its sharp hooked beak. Screeching as its wings caught Prometheus in the face, it continued its meal, digging deeper into his flesh with each triumphant cry.

Without hope or ability to free himself, Prometheus wept with anguished heaving of the shoulders, watching as the bird reached his liver and began ripping it from his body. When the pain was undoubtedly at its peak, Prometheus again felt the impending darkness as he fainted.

Waking with a scream and a jolt, he shuddered as he looked to where the eagle had attacked him but gasped aloud to see his flesh untorn, precisely as it had always been. There was no eagle, no deadly talons or shredding beak. Was it a dream? The Titan sighed in relief.

The feeling was short-lived, though, as the same awful pain caused him to try and lurch to one side only to be held firm by his restraints. The eagle was back and began devouring his side with the same fervor as before. It engulfed every chunk of flesh as it tore deep down to the liver. Again Prometheus strained and cried out to no avail. Again, darkness took him, and then again he woke to skin without flaw, and no eagle present to feast on him. Within moments, however, it all began again with renewed pain and suffering.

Zeus had decided, for so great was the betrayal of Prometheus that only an eternal consequence would suffice. Day after day, morning found the Titan still chained and unharmed, but soon enough, he would be torn asunder at the mercy of the great eagle. No matter how loudly he cried out, it would never end. An infinite loop of pain and suffering would torment Prometheus for eternity.

Generations passed, each one identical to the last for Prometheus, filled with horrors and torture. Then one day, a wandering hero happened to be passing by the rock upon which the Titan was shackled.

Having no strength to signal the passerby, Prometheus hung in despair. Suddenly the eagle let out a screeching squawk that he had not heard before, and then another. Finding the courage to look about, Prometheus noticed the beating wings fall away as the eagle was showered with piercing arrows. With a final cry, it fell into the sea below. With joyful sobs, hardly believing it to be real, Prometheus looked up into the face of his savior, who shattered the chains with a few heavy blows.

Setting the beaten Titan on the ground to rest, the hero nodded and turned to go his way.

"Wait." Prometheus's voice was weak from little use over the years, "What is the name of the hero that rescued me from my endless torment?"

With a humble look on his face, the hero answered with one word and then continued on his journey.

"Heracles."

CHAPTER TWO:

PANDORA AND HER JAR

Zeus felt betrayed by Prometheus, someone he had considered a close cohort. Side by side, they had gone into the fray during the war with the Titans, and yet it had all come to this. The leader of the gods was in a foul mood atop Mount Olympus while the Titan of fire was chained to a rock in the midst of his eternal punishment. Zeus had gotten his revenge against the immortal who turned against him, but what of those who Prometheus sought to aid? The gift of fire had awakened humanity, and with it, Zeus felt his power begin to weaken.

While Zeus was mighty, the emotions that ran hot in his veins would often get the better of him, and this situation would be no different. Despite the pettiness of his thoughts, everything was focused on getting back at those humans who learned the gods' secret of fire. It wasn't enough for him to have a hand in it, for his anger delved deep into the darkest parts of himself.

Calling the other gods to his side, Zeus informed each of them of his expectations and desires for mankind, and, without much choice, they complied. Zeus had already punished Prometheus, and so to attain his vengeance on humanity, he would instead target Epimetheus, the brother of Prometheus, who had also fought beside the gods in the Titan war. After some deliberation, the gods would decide on using trickery of many sorts as a means of infiltrating the human world.

It was Hephaestus who was given the task of creating the object of their trickery; a woman. From the clay atop Olympus, the blacksmith god formed her in utter perfection. She was beautiful, and the mere glimpse of her shape beckoned the hearts of men. Next, Zeus called Athena to bestow the gifts of crafts and art to ensnare men's minds further. Aphrodite was after her, and with a single touch, she filled the woman's form with femininity and charm. Every wile and angle at a woman's disposal was offered in full to the figure before them. Lastly, Hermes came forward, and - after being forced by Zeus's hand, whispered the secrets of deception and curiosity into the woman's ears. His voice carried through her and taught her well.

Once woman had been formed to perfection, Zeus looked over this creation and just knew it to be the perfect addition to enact his revenge as he intended, but there was more to do. He gently brushed the woman's forehead, and her eyes gently opened to show the purest look the world had ever seen. She looked around her and then to Zeus with a curious gaze.

"Welcome to life, Pandora," whispered Zeus, placing a hand lightly on her cheek. "You are of great importance to this universe, for soon I shall take you to the world of humans where you will meet the man who shall be your spouse. He is a great and true man, a powerful Titan, who will be overcome by your beauty and forever shall you live in peace and joy."

Upon hearing these words, Pandora lit up with glee and nodded her approval. It sounded so exhilarating, and she couldn't wait to meet this man and begin a life such as the one Zeus described.

It wasn't long before Zeus assembled his traveling party and descended Olympus with Pandora beside him. Through forests and over peaks they went, drawing stares and whispers wherever they trekked. All eyes were focused on Pandora, despite the convoy of immortals and gods beside her. Impressive as they were, nothing shined brighter than the woman standing beside Zeus.

"Where is this man you spoke of?" asked Pandora. "Where is my husband, great Zeus?"

"Soon, you shall be presented to him," Zeus reassured her, "and then all shall come to pass as I said. Not long now." She settled back and was patient for the remainder of the journey, for she had no reason to doubt the words of her creator.

Finally, after many miles traversed, they came to the small town where Epimetheus resided. The whole community was full of commotion as they saw the group nearing the town. With a wary look on his face, the Titan stepped forward to see what all the commotion was about. Prometheus warned his brother many times about accepting gifts from the gods, as it always came with a price. These words echoed in Epimetheus's mind as he nodded toward Zeus, but then he felt his breath suddenly taken away. Never before had he seen anything so beautiful.

Zeus gently helped Pandora forward toward the Titan and feigned reverence as he spoke.

"Epimetheus, the revered brother of Prometheus, do not think that I have forgotten all you have done for me," Zeus's voice thundered so that all could hear. "You turned your back on your kind for the sake of this world, and it is for this loyalty that I have come to you this day.

"I considered many rewards that would fit this incredible courage, but in all this world, I could not find anything that measured up to the level of your bravery. Because of this, I chose to use my power, and from the clay of the earth itself, the gods have formed this woman for you to take as your wife. I present to you, Pandora."

Pandora saw Zeus nod to her, and so she made a curtsey before Epimetheus, nervous and unsure about how she would be received. Her heart was aflutter with hope for all the things Zeus had promised, but the Titan stood in utter disbelief. After a few moments of heavy silence, Epimetheus found his words.

"I have lived many, many years and seen almost all manner of things, but never before have I laid eyes on something as beautiful as you, dear woman."

This brought a flush of red to Pandora's face, and she curtseyed even lower.

"I'm glad that I am pleasing to you." Pandora's voice was shaky, but she was determined to show her best self. "You shall have my loyalty and love, and my life is yours for as long as the gods and fates allow."

This brought a great cheer from the crowd, and Zeus knew that his plan was beginning to blossom. With raised arms and a large grin on his face, the god spoke to all that were gathered there.

"Let us waste no time, for these two desire to begin their lives together." Every word echoed across the expanse, reaching every person from the town. "It shall be a wedding unlike any other!"

Another roar of approval erupted from the crowd, and they all dispersed in a spark of joy and merriment in preparation for the festivities.

It was indeed a wedding like no other; wine flowing freely, music and dancing, food on every surface in every form imaginable. Everywhere you looked, there were cheerful faces and toasts to the new couple. Among all the chaos, Zeus took Pandora away for a walk someplace quiet where they could talk.

"It is tradition for the bride to receive a gift," Zeus told her, "and I would be honored to present you with this." He handed Pandora a beautifully ornate clay jar.

What seemed like a beautiful piece of craftsmanship on the outside, was in fact, a treacherous artifact that Zeus had prepared to carry out revenge against humanity. It was no ordinary jar, for inside existed every horrible thing that the gods could think up. Disease, pain, calamity, death, and every other dark feeling or action was contained within the confines of the exquisite jar. It all came as a surprise to Pandora who could only thank the gods that blessed her indeed to be living a life such as this.

"Oh, mighty Zeus," Pandora fawned over her gift, "I shall treasure this gift for every day of my life. Every time my eyes fall upon it, I shall remember the kindness you showed me."

Zeus nodded to her and then leaned in to whisper.

"Be wary, dear Pandora," he said in a cautious tone. "Though it is beautiful on the outside, you must never look inside. I cannot tell you why, but never allow your curiosity to get the better of you, lest my warnings go by the wayside."

"Of course," she exclaimed. "I shall never dream of peeking inside, not even once!"

Zeus smiled at this answer, for though he appeared to delight in her self-control, he knew the depth of what Hermes had given to Pandora and that it would not take long for her nature to get the best of her, despite her intentions. She was, after all, created for destruction.

In the days following the wedding, Pandora and Epimetheus were happier than ever thought possible. Their future seemed to stretch into eternal joy, and nothing dampened their moods. Every day Pandora would walk past the jar and remember the words of Zeus, and at first, it helped her determination to remain faithful to her word, but each time after, it began to chisel away at her fortitude. She didn't even notice as she began to let her mind drift to wondering what was within that jar, despite the warnings Zeus himself had given her. She was embattled in a daily struggle between her desire to honor her promise and the curiosity that Hermes had filled her with. Paths such as this tend to continue moving toward the darker side of humanity, and Pandora was no different. As strong as her moral urges were, the true reason she was created was winning more small battles each day until she found herself with her hands trembling, just inches from the lid of the jar.

Walk away, Pandora. Her thoughts were doing their best to steer her in the right direction, but she felt her will deteriorating quickly. *You can do it, just stop and walk away.*

It was as though her mind was telling her the exact opposite, because she felt the cool ceramic beneath her fingers as she was now holding the jar in her grasp. Her breath was shaky and uncertain. Almost in a trance, she held the jar in one arm, and the other hand crept slowly toward the lid. There was something electric in the air as she felt around the crease and toyed with the engravings for a moment.

Please don't. Please don't, she begged herself over and over, tears starting to cascade down her face. Her eyes were wide and scared as she watched her fingers, independent of her thoughts, begin to work the lid back and forth, hearing the light scrape of pottery as it started to loosen.

There's still time, put it back, there's—

Her thought was violently interrupted when the lid popped. Before anything else could happen, the room was filled with wind, rushing movement, screams, evil faces, and at the center of it all was a weeping woman holding an open jar. With frail arms, she fought to shut the jar again, but it was too late by the time she finally forced it closed. She thought it was lucky that something was still confined inside because maybe that meant the worst hadn't happened, but sadly that was not the case.

Lost among the evils and terrible things within the jar, Hope itself had been trapped inside. Desperate to free itself, Hope fought toward the opening when it was ajar, but before it could escape, the lid slammed back down, trapping it again.

There was nothing more Pandora could do except collapse into a sorrowful heap. Zeus had told her precisely what *not* to do, and yet everything had gone wrong so quickly. Nothing could console her, even her husband, who was distraught when he learned of what had transpired. From that point onward, the world of humans was never free from evil. Swift and terrible was the consequence of Pandora's actions, purposeful or not.

Some say that Hope found a small crack in the jar and escaped as well, desperately trying to repair the chaos that evil caused in the world. Others say that Hope is still trapped in the jar, guarded forever by Pandora so that she shall never open it again. Only the gods know the truth.

Chapter Three:

The Myth of Narcissus and Echo

The wondrous land of Greece is one in which water plays quite a vital role. Sweeping coasts on either side, deep lakes and rivers abound; in fact, all the kingdoms of Greece are islands, and the sea is their livelihood. All this is brought to life by the gracious touch of Cephissus, a god of the rivers. One day this river god noticed a fountain nymph nearby and fell for her beauty and spirit. Her name was Liriope. By day they would frolic amongst the waters, and by night they found love with each other. It wasn't long before Liriope learned that she was with child, and her joy grew all the more for it.

All children are beautiful, but any born before and born after would pale compared to the first glowing child birthed by the nymph. The young mother had never before seen such utter perfection, and it took her breath away. She knew in the depths of herself that there was no limit to what she would do to ensure that her child—her perfect, untainted boy—would never be harmed. How though, with life such as it was, would a mother *truly* be able to protect her child from all the dangers of this world?

As nymphs do, she knew of a seer that had sight far beyond that of this realm, and his name was Tiresias. In secret, she journeyed to seek his counsel as to how she might stave off the fates and save her child from a mortal end. Tiresias welcomed her and the child, though when he looked upon Narcissus and bore witness to the sheer beauty of the boy, he too—despite the long life he had lived, and all he had seen—knew that the child's mother was right in wanting to do all within her power to protect such a gift.

"There is but one way to be sure beyond doubt that he is shielded from harm," the seer spoke gently, though there was assurance behind his words. "Never let this child see himself. If ever his eyes look upon his perfection, the warding shall be lifted, and all manner of harm and evil shall be allowed to befall him."

His mother wailed and wept upon the swaddling that wrapped her child, but the seer calmed her and spoke strength. The wise old seer knew the power of a mother's love and saw the same in Liriope's gaze. He bid her to raise this child well and with honor, but above all to abide by the words he had spoken over Narcissus.

While Narcissus was not able to look on himself, the world around him had no reason not to fawn over a child with such glorious features as his. From the moment Liriope began carrying him around, every person would stop and gasp at such a beauteous baby. From infant to teenager, Narcissus grew and every year brought more depth to his handsomeness and more suitors to his doorstep. Each one would swear their very lives to him if he would only love them. None succeeded in swaying him, for, in truth, he had never once felt love for another creature. He had affection for his dear mother, but nothing like what these men and women were showing him.

Many were turned away, but one, in particular, stood out among the masses, a youth called Ameinias. Viral, passionate, and charming were all accurate descriptions of Ameinias, and if there were a second to Narcissus, it would have been him. The youth could have had his choice of anyone in any place he desired to go, and yet he spent every single day desperately trying to woo Narcissus. Serenades in the moonlight, expensive perfumes, and gifts—nothing caught the attention of this stunning man, much to the heartache of Ameinias.

Finally, the young man decided that a grand gesture would surely gain him the affections of this much-sought-after man. Ameinias waited until Narcissus took a walk through the usually crowded streets of Boeotian, and once there were enough people, he made a complete spectacle of himself. Screaming his love and undying devotion to Narcissus, Ameinias threw himself onto the rock-strewn ground and lay weeping, reaching for merely a touch of his sandals, anything to be noticed by this splendid creature. It was all for nothing, Narcissus stepped around the prostrate youth and continued on with no interest in the recent episode.

Narcissus may have never felt the pang of love, but he certainly felt irritation and the desire for this persistent fawning to cease. Others had come and gone, but this particular one, Ameinias, was becoming more and more akin to a thorn than a flower. Narcissus set in motion a scheme dark in tone and malicious in nature with the desire to be rid of these affections.

Ameinias discovered a wrapped parcel in front of his dwelling early the following day with an ornate note attached. Expecting something joyous to lift his spirits, Ameinias opened the gift to find a gleaming sword within and the message reading the following:

You have sworn time and time over that if I wished it so, your life would be mine.
Now I wish it so. Thus I give you this final gift to remove from this earth what is my right to remove; your life.

So great was the heartbreak this brought on that Ameinias heard it crack within his chest. With the horrible weapon in hand, he trudged to the doorstep of Narcissus and, with a loud cry, split himself apart in a blood-filled fury. The blade clattered to the ground, and Narcissus's desire to be free of Ameinias was complete. Still, standing over the bleeding body of the youth, Narcissus felt nothing, neither guilt nor shame.

Wanting to clear his mind after the ordeal with Ameinias, Narcissus went deep into the woods. He hoped that by bringing his spirit back to nature, he could find some peace and perhaps the love he had never before felt.

As he wandered through the forest, winding between trees and breathing in the rich air, he heard a sound that he could have sworn was a giggle. Turning all about, he saw nothing, and the sound could no longer be heard, so he continued his walk. A few minutes later, he heard a rustling in the trees.

"Aye!" shouted Narcissus, eyes darting around from tree to tree. "There's no need to hide. Please, show yourself."

Echo answered him with silence.

Not wanting to miss a chance, he stood still for a brief moment, but the trees remained motionless. It wasn't until he sighed and continued through the woods that he heard the noise again. This time he stopped entirely and made sure his tone was much less pleasant than before.

"Show yourself! You will gain nothing from hiding!"

This time, he got a response. *"You will gain nothing from hiding!"*

It sounded like his own voice thrown back at him, only it seemed further off and hollow. Taking a step back and uneasily looking all about, he tried again.

"Who is there?" he demanded.

"Who is there?" it repeated back, just as before.

"Come out!" he shouted, louder still, unsure of which direction to face lest he end up yelling at the trees alone.

"Come out." Echoed out.

Narcissus had no more desire to discover the voice owner and instead sought to escape it by trudging even deeper into the forest. After several minutes of weaving and ducking, he figured that he had successfully evaded whatever had aimed to torment him. Staying as quiet as he could, Narcissus peered around, trying to discern any movement that wasn't caused by the wind. He let a few more minutes pass, and then, in almost a whisper, he spoke.

"Are you still there?"

"Are you still there?"

The response caused Narcissus to throw his hands in the air in exasperation. Expecting more of the same, he turned all about but was taken aback when a small mountain nymph stepped from behind the trees and stared at him.

Narcissus saw only the nymph before him, but he was not aware of what had driven her this far into the woods, mountain folk as she was. She was no ordinary nymph; this was Echo, who was punished for protecting Zeus from the wrath of his suspicious wife, Hera. In her jealous rage, Hera had cursed the nymph only ever to repeat what was said to her and nothing more. Abandoned by Zeus and despised by Hera,

Echo retreated into the forest where she remained hidden and alone until that very moment when she chose to step into the light. To step toward Narcissus.

It is a sad day indeed when one expectation is dashed upon another. When Echo chose to reveal herself, it was unfortunate that the one she chose was Narcissus, an unfeeling man who only knew how to spurn affection. In all her days, Echo had not seen anything as beautiful as this man who had been walking through her woods, and yet here he was. She was coy and shy, hiding behind the trees and calling back to him. Narcissus, however, was anything but pleased at yet another admirer coming from the woodwork to seek his attention. He had come here to escape this very moment, and yet it was happening once again.

Echo began slowly pacing toward Narcissus from the tree line, her eyes wary and movements purposeful. Where she showed curiosity, he was rigid and skeptical. Finally, she allowed herself to get right up next to him, but only silence followed when she opened her mouth to speak. With wide, desperate eyes, she reached for him, mouth open but no words spilling forth.

"Stop. What are you doing?" With a squirming motion, he pushed her advances away, not meeting her stare.

"Stop. What are you doing?" Her voice was cracked, as though something beneath the words was trying to get out, but all Narcissus heard was the same frustrations as before.

He threw her from him with a strong heave, her slight form crumpling on the forest floor. As he turned away from her, he could hear the sobs start to shake her body, but still, the only singular emotion within him was the same irritation as before. It remained the same; they wanted love and affection, but they sparked nothing within him, nothing positive at least. Where he had hoped for mutual feelings, he found a desert that held nothing but disappointment. With these jaded thoughts, he left the nymph, Echo, weeping into the fallen leaves.

Throw a stone into a pond, and the ripples will spread to the furthest bank. In the world, when one action occurs, it is never isolated, and this is how it was with Echo. As Narcissus departed, cruelly leaving her to fend for herself despite the vulnerability she had shown, there was another pair of eyes watching over the sorrowful nymph. The goddess of revenge, Nemesis, recognized the repeating calls that came from the forest, and on this particular day, there was a different energy. It was no longer just the usual call and response. This time there was passion and curiosity behind the words Echo repeated back, and Nemesis desired to know why.

It didn't take the goddess long to discern why she had felt a shift in Echo's energy. Narcissus didn't just stand out to mortals. Even in the realm of the gods, he was an impressive specimen, but his glorious appearance was no match for the concern Nemesis felt for the nymph. Perhaps it took the vision of an immortal, but Nemesis saw underneath the shining exterior to a hard, cruel underbelly that tended to be at the reins.

She watched it all unfold—the chase, the refusal by Narcissus, and the carnage of heartbreak left behind. Filled with the anger and power that Echo did not have the capacity for, the goddess set out to find Narcissus and ensure that no one would be caused pain by his unfeeling actions again. Even as Nemesis began her chase, she could hear the cries of Echo deadening as distance parted them. The heartbreak was slowly killing the nymph; this added fire to the belly of the goddess as she hastened her quest.

Within a few hours, Nemesis had tracked Narcissus to a more sparse forest to the east. Concealing herself behind a cluster of trees, she waited until he wandered past and leaped out directly into his path.

"Narcissus!" she thundered, her form glowing and seeming to rise before him.

Trembling, he fell to his knees, recognizing a goddess when she appeared. He held his hands before his face, fearing the holy light shining around her.

"Narcissus," again she called, "I have heard from the nymph, Echo, that you spurned her advances."

He nodded, having no reason to lie to her.

"Indeed, oh goddess," Narcissus said shakily. "In all my days, I have not felt affection for another, let alone those who have pursued me. And so, like the others, I cast her aside."

She bristled at his lack of compassion but held her composure. Nemesis had heard tell of the magical words spoken over him by the seer, as gods and goddess gossip among the others without fail, and she mustered up a plan.

"What a tragic thing, indeed, for someone such as you to be without love. Even worse, to be sought after by those you feel nothing for."

"It has been near torture, dear goddess. I have felt nothing but disappointment. To feel anything more would be a dream come true."

Those words he spoke let Nemesis know that her plot was sure to succeed, all she needed to do was reel in the bait, and Narcissus would willingly follow.

"I nearly forgot!" exclaimed Nemesis. "Not far from here, I saw another like you; glorious in beauty and perfect without fail. If you let me lead you, you may find those affections sooner than you think!"

Narcissus agreed and followed close behind the goddess with a gleeful sound as she led him through the forest toward the trap up ahead.

When they were several paces from the calm waters, Nemesis stopped and turned to Narcissus.

"Now, be quiet and cautious, for this is a shy one, who will flee if approached quickly."

"Of course, I shall tiptoe so that she hears nothing of my footsteps."

"Perfect, that is precisely how you should proceed." Nemesis knew how close she was to exacting revenge for all this man's transgressions. A few more well-placed words, and it would all be in motion. "After a few steps, peer over the bushes and there your match will be revealed to you."

Narcissus nodded and turned his attention to the instructions he had been given. Being as quiet as he could, he crept to the bush and carefully peeked over the leaves to behold this spectacle of beauty that had been promised him. What met his gaze was indeed and without a doubt as perfect a being as he had ever seen. Not one thing was uneven or out of place, from the flowing hair to the flawless skin. He moved closer still until he was lying on the bank beside the pond, staring into the eyes of the only thing he had ever felt love for. With a deep sigh, he knew that he could stay forever in this spot. For Narcissus had found his eternal love.

The hours passed, and so did the days; all the while, Narcissus stayed at the edge of the water. Not once did he turn his eyes from the beauteous image in the pond. So devoted was the man to his newfound love that Narcissus put any thought of food or drink far from his mind. Each sunset found Narcissus thinner and thinner, his eyes sunken but steadfast on the water.

After many days had passed, the emaciated figure by the pond's edge lifted his head for the last time to ensure he didn't lose sight of his beloved. Gathering what strength he had left, Narcissus put it all into his final words.

"My love, long I sought you, and now you are mine forever. Farewell, my love." And his head slumped forward as death came for Narcissus.

Across the water, hidden from view, the tear-filled eyes of Echo watched the man give up his life and depart from this world. In the only voice she had, the nymph spoke.

"Farewell, my love."

Chapter Four:

King Midas and His Golden Touch

In a time of great wealth and peace, there spread a land called Phrygia, green and rich from one border to the next. It was within this wondrous region that a greed stricken king named Midas reigned, and did so with much joy amongst all of his affluence. From the sprawling courtyards to the lustrous walls surrounding the palace, there were signs of the king's love of luxury wherever one would care to look.

If Midas's life wasn't already a blessed one, he had one treasure that was greater and more dear to him than anything in the kingdom; his daughter, Zoe. Though the king had his mind often on the wealth around him, and how to accumulate more, she was more precious to him than any stockpile or gemstone. While these feelings for his daughter were entrenched deep within his heart, he did not always express these affections as often or directly as he should. It was for this reason that his daughter had often wondered which her father loved more, herself or his riches.

The rule of king Midas was during the time of mystics and Olympus. As the gods tended to do, infighting and deviance were commonplace in the nearby countries, and so it was that the god Dionysus, was leading his followers and companions to Thrace to indulge themselves in wine, food, and pleasure. He was surrounded by all sorts and manner of creatures and beings; satyrs, nymphs, alongside so many more, all journeying together toward the festivities and celebrations. In all the bustle that happens in a crowd that large, Dionysus seemed to have lost track of his dearest companion; the satyr, Silenus. Soon after they had reached Thrace, Dionysus realized that his beloved satyr was in fact missing entirely from the group and must have fell behind on their expedition.

"Who saw him last?" the god's voice echoed across the crowd. "Where is my cohort? Where is Silenus?" It was to no avail, though, and it was with a heavy heart that Dionysus continued to search for the missing satyr.

What had happened to this old and loved one? During the festivities that occur when a group such as theirs were together, drink was plentiful, and Silenus partook in every chance possible. It didn't take long for the wine to rush to his head and cause him to stumble into a nearby garden, where he felt the full impact of his drinking. It wasn't a moment later that the satyr was fast asleep in a bed of flowers, and this is where the tale would have ended if not for the whereabouts of that particular garden where the satyr set his drunken head. It was not just any bed of flowers, nor any courtyard, that he was in; it all belonged to the king of Phrygia, King Midas.

The hours passed, and it was nearing midnight when a trio of peasants from Phrygia were strolling through the outer region of the gardens. For all the cheerful chatter and carrying on that the three men did, it was a wonder that they noticed anything at all, but one of them stopped short and pointed to the figure passed out in the sunflower patch.

"Do you two know who that is?" he asked, squinting in the dim moonlight, steadying himself on his two companions. The men did their best to look on either side of him, but their evening's activities mixed with the darkness hindered their vision. It took a few moments for the men to make their way over the flower bed, but their eyes grew wide when they did.

"Is it the drink, or is this a satyr, my friends?" the middle man asked, briskly rubbing his eyes.

"If it's the drink, it's hitting me the same."

"Me as well, for that is certainly a satyr asleep there."

Now that the three agreed on what creature lay before them, they realized that they needed to do something about the situation.

"Should we wake him?" the middle man, asked. He seemed nervous, as superstitious men were apt to be. His two friends were equally superstitious, if not more, and so they too seemed uneasy in the presence of Silenus. While it was not uncommon to hear of the gods carrying on throughout the lands, being this close to one, let alone seeing a satyr this vulnerable, was different altogether.

"Don't wake him, for who knows how a satyr reacts upon being woken?"

"Too, true. You know who *would* know what to do with him?" the third man asked, looking at his two companions. They nodded. The answer was obvious to them, as it would have been to anyone in Phrygia. King Midas would know what to do.

None of the three men had ever laid eyes on a satyr, let alone carried one, but they were still awfully wary of how one might respond to waking up in transit. The panic of a mystical creature feeling threatened could instigate catastrophic damage. It was for this reason that King Midas found himself being roused from his sleep, hurried to the throne room, and presented with one of the most curious sights he had ever witnessed. Standing before him were three men, swaying slightly and reeking of wine, but in front of them, secured with vines, was a very old satyr, seeming to be worse off in drink than any of the three who had bound him.

"What is the meaning of this?" shouted Midas, rushing to the creature and immediately removing the vines from its arms and legs. "What reason could you have to bind a creature such as this? Do you not know that the gods look favorably upon those like him? How do you think they would view men who bound one of their favorite beings?"

The king was rearing up to continue his tirade when a small voice stopped him. He looked down and saw that the satyr was fully awake and speaking.

"Be calm, King Midas, for they were acting as men do, with fear, but without malice."

As Silenus stood and brushed himself off, he made a slight bow before Midas and then to the three men, all of whom were looking more confused than anything.

"Truth be told, I am responsible for this entire circumstance, for I got myself separated from my party and my friends when the drink hit me fully." He laughed and shrugged. "These men were doing the best they could, considering their worry. If they were of the bad sort, I surely wouldn't be standing before you now, and so I thank them. I am standing in a grand palace; if they had not taken me, I would still be asleep on your sunflowers, oh king."

These words brought pause to the king's anger, and he thought it over before speaking again.

"Far be it for a mere man to question the voice of you, oh satyr." He turned to the three peasants. "To you men, I thank you for putting our land in the good graces of this wonderful creature. I ask you to stay and partake as we feast to celebrate our honored and most unexpected guest."

Then to the satyr, he turned and spoke. "And to you, satyr, my friend, would you stay and feast with us? Enjoy our wealth and happiness, and then I shall accompany you to wherever you call home."

A joyous reply of agreeance came from the four in question. The three peasants appeared thrilled that they were not in any trouble, and the court was again impressed with how their king had handled the situation. As the palace began preparing for the upcoming festivities, King Midas took the satyr aside to speak plainly.

"I apologize, dear satyr," Midas said, "but I do not know by what name I should call you. Nor do I know where you hail from and where I should help you return to."

"My name is Silenus," the old satyr explained, "and I have long traveled with Dionysus and his party, though this time I did not heed the drink, and it got the better of me. It has happened before, but never to the extent where I woke without him nearby. I would never turn down your heartfelt hospitality, and once we have eaten and drunk our fill, we shall set out to find my friend and kin, Dionysus."

The festivity, feasting and celebrating, was as glorious as you might expect when a satyr and a king are at the heads of the table. For ten days, they drank and ate, toasting gods and mystics alike. When the boisterous activities were nearing conclusion, the king decided it was time to set out and return Silenus to Dionysus, where both king and satyr hoped even more celebration would ensue.

It was around this time that word arrived at the palace that Dionysus had moved his party to Lydia, where he was still frantically waiting for Silenus to find his way back to them. With news of Dionysus' whereabouts King Midas set off to return Silenus back to his dear friend. Not wanting to give the god any cause to flee, the king kept their traveling company small, and in only a few days, they reached the brightly colored tents that dotted the camp of Dionysus. It only took a few moments before the kings men began to hear a booming voice thunder toward them.

"Have I heard correctly?" The depth of Dionysus's voice carried to every corner of the encampment. "Has my dear kin been returned to me?"

For all the wondrous things that King Midas had seen in all his days, for all the extravagance in his palace and throughout the kingdom, he had never before seen something as glorious and vibrantly alive as this god lumbering toward them. Standing well over seven feet, he somehow didn't loom over anyone but instead made all near him feel at ease. A vibrant red robe swept around his large frame; even the folds and creases in the fabric seemed to add to the wonder of it all. His head was woven with leaves and grapevines, some with perfectly ripe, purple fruit almost holding itself in a still-life for the god. It was a sight to behold indeed, from his sandaled feet to the top of his curly head of hair, and this left Midas without words for one of the first times in his life.

"My dear friend, it is me." Silenus bowed in front of the god and motioned toward Midas, still unsure how to act or even breathe. "For though I got lost in drink, I was found in the hospitality of this honorable king."

"Is this true, oh king?" Dionysus asked, staring down Midas, who could only nod and bow further. At this, the god let out a full laugh and smiled. "This is truly a wondrous thing that you have done for me. What is the name of such a king who would return a friend as dear as Silenus to my side?"

"Me?" Midas managed to gasp out, still shaken by the mere presence of a being as powerful and magnificent as Dionysus. Another rumble of laughter shook the air.

"Unless there is another king responsible for my joy, I do mean, you, yes."

"My name is Midas, oh great Dionysus. I am the King of Phrygia." And despite being nearly on his knees, he tried to bow lower, shakily balancing. The god motioned for him to stand, which he immediately did. Dionysus turned to all those who had gathered to see what the commotion was all about.

"Friends and those among us, hear this!" Dionysus put his hands up, nodding toward Midas. "You all know how distraught I have been over this missing companion of mine, Silenus." The crowd sadly murmured acknowledgment. "Do not be sad, for my news is joyous! Today is one for rejoicing, because here stands Silenus; returned and home!"

A cheer erupted from within the entire camp.

"There is more, dear ones!" He soothed them down before continuing, motioning for Midas to approach him. "Here is the one responsible for the safe and welcome return of my dearest friend. I present to you, King Midas!"

If the sound of the crowd seemed loud before, this next cheer became deafening. All focus was on the king, who now stood before the god, wondering what was next. "Because of what you have done, I shall grant you one request, whatever is dear to your heart. Ask, and it shall be yours."

When Midas heard this, it filled his mind with possibilities; wisdom, power, it all swirled before him, now attainable instead of mere desires. At the core of all was one thing: gold and riches. Among all things that he could want, that was always first and foremost. He never seemed to have enough and now was his chance to *never* worry about that ever again. He took a deep breath for courage, and, standing as straight and tall as he could, he answered Dionysus.

"While there are many things in this world that I could ask for," King Midas declared, "there is only one that I know will fulfill my deepest desires and finally bring contentment and lasting joy to myself and my kingdom forever. For as long as I can remember, I have devoted my rule and my life to accumulating as much wealth as possible, never stopping for fear that it may not be enough.

"Even as a child, I would observe the ants scurrying about in their world far below, and no matter the heat or rain, they kept about their duties—each one dedicated to building up the colony's stockpile. I drew inspiration from their example, and with an ant's work ethic, I also devoted myself to building the kingdom and its riches to new heights. It is for all of these reasons that my mind and heart have agreed on a single request from you, oh great Dionysus.

"While asking for chests of treasure would be fruitful, it is a single moment and may not be enough. I ask that you bless me, that anything I touch would turn to gold."

To the king, this seemed a sage choice indeed, but his request pained the heart of Dionysus, for he knew the depth of consequence that comes from such greed. While the king before him now was one of goodness and truth, this gift would surely dim that glow of righteousness. He had given his word, though, and for such an undertaking as returning Silenus, he would grant even a foolish wish.

"You shall have what you ask for, King Midas," Dionysus decreed, his voice firm but filled with sorrow. "It is done."

Midas was expecting more pageantry or flourish, and so he was slightly skeptical about the result.

"It's done? That's it?" he questioned, looking himself over as if something physical would change to indicate the power for which he had asked. No cloud of magic, no sound or enchantment to be heard.

"It is, oh Midas," Silenus asserted, ever protecting the god to whom he swore his life. "Here, if you are unsure, observe your touch on this branch."

The satyr held out a short branch with several small leaves. Midas looked at the branch and held his hand out, almost afraid and reluctant to put this to the test. Finally, his finger met the branch, and with a brilliant shine, a golden overlay covered the branch in which he had just touched. Like running water, it flowed up and around the length of the stick, then up to each stem onto the leaves until the entire branch gleamed of gold. An audible gasp came not only from Midas himself but from all those who had journeyed with him from the palace. They had heard of the power the gods possessed, but for their king to have turned a plain, leafy branch into a shining, golden stick was more than they thought possible.

"You spoke the truth! Truly this is the most marvelous thing to happen since time began!"

Dionysus gave a sad nod in recognition of the king's words but then turned away along with Silenus. So great was the king's joy that he barely noticed when the camp packed up, and before long, it was only the king and his men left standing in the open field. He was so caught up in turning individual blades of grass into gold that he did not even notice the gods departure.

All the journey back to the kingdom, Midas spent his time turning everything he could see and reach into solid gold. Each time he gave a gleeful squeal, clapping his hands, then would repeat the whole process again. Anyone could have followed the company of men due to the shimmering trail of gold marking their path. The king's followers grew in unease at the freedom with which Midas was exercising his new touch, but they had obeyed his rule before, and they didn't see this as anything to be overly concerned about… yet. Worry or not, he was their king, and that was what mattered.

Soon they were back home, and the entire palace and surrounding regions were curious to hear about the king's quest to return Silenus to Dionysus. Still, no one could have expected what had occurred. Some mistrusted such a gift, while others believed it would establish their kingdom the unquestionable ruler over all others.

Whatever their opinions were, the empire was celebrating Midas' return, and so the palace ordered a grand feast. As he had done on countless occasions, the king took a stroll through his gardens in wait of the festivities. The colors were always a wondrous sight to behold, and this time was no different; the reds of the rose, yellows in the sunflowers, every petal and leaf a welcome addition to the final picture of beauty. It didn't need to be improved, yet the king saw with a new perspective; if it wasn't gold, why not turn it into gold?

With this in mind, he went all about the courtyards and gardens, fingers touching here and there as he saw fit; red to gold, green to gold, violet to gold; it all transformed before his eyes, just as incredible as the first branch he had touched.

He couldn't wait to show his daughter the new and beautiful skill he had recently acquired. Never again would he have to lose focus or time with her by seeking treasure because wherever he was, he could now create it. Surely she would see the wonder and value in this as well, and so he continued his golden walk, genuinely believing that every touch brought him closer to happiness that would never fade.

That evening, the extensive celebration had commenced, and countless faces sat at the tables, all eager to lay eyes on their powerful, wealth-birthing king. When he emerged and was seated at the middle of the central table, he stood and waited for the voices to die down before raising both arms toward them.

"My subjects, those from far and those nearby, welcome to an occasion never before witnessed in either our kingdom or time! For I have returned from meeting with none other than the god Dionysus, to whom I helped return his dearest companion, the satyr, Silenus."

At this, the masses let loose with impressed murmurs, which slowly calmed so Midas could continue.

"If the honor of being in the presence of a god was not enough, he offered to grant a single request as a gift for the safe return of Silenus. I would need all my wisdom to make the right choice, and I have been blessed by the hands of a god!"

With his voice rising in volume, he reached down and grabbed the large goblet before him, a polished silver. The whole room gasped and began talking openly as the cup transformed into the same gold as everything else the king had touched. Midas lifted the now-golden goblet to the court and put it to his lips with a proud grin. Something was wrong because what should have felt like the splash of rich liquid, there was nothing but the taste of cold metal. He pulled the cup away from his mouth to see that the drink within was now a motionless lump of gold, just as the cup itself was. Trying to remain calm, the king smiled at his subjects and reached for another goblet, this one also turning to gold. In a hurried rush the king lifted the goblet to his lips, wanting to beat the golden touch. Unfortunately, as you may have guessed, the same thing happened, and yet another glassful of wine malformed into a hunk of gold.

Over and over, he tried and failed to drink, and his panic only increased as he tried to eat. He first attempted with a chicken leg, but the instant he wrenched it from the carcass, it was a gleaming drumstick, the same with the stew and pastries. What had started as a joyful celebration was now a fear-stricken catastrophe in which the subjects watched their king wander from table to table, crying out as each attempt to bite into meat and bread alike was met with a pained clang and the king tossing another piece of golden food aside.

"Don't let the king's touch reach you!" someone in the crowd yelled, and with the terror that was building, that was all that was needed for the panic to strike fully. In a blur of screams and feet, the court emptied itself, its fearful inhabitants now running to anywhere that the king was not. One person remained behind to comfort her crying father, and this was his daughter, Zoe. She was at a distance, but she shouted peaceful words to him as he slowly crept closer.

"My daughter, my beloved, Zoe, fear not," he said, though his tone was unsure. "Surely the gods would not push this torment so far that my arms could not hold you. You shall be safe, my dear, for though I have always desired to be surrounded by gold, you have been beyond improvement in perfection, so nothing shall happen."

She looked at him with trusting eyes and held her arms out toward him. As he approached, she closed her eyes, arms still outstretched. To his horror, though, the moment he felt his arms around his daughter, she became motionless as well. He felt her once-warm skin, and it was the same awful, lifeless metal that now surrounded him. He dared not pull away, for he knew what he would gaze upon, and the mere thought was breaking his heart within his chest.

"Zoe, my daughter, please speak," he begged, arms still tightly clasped around the golden girl. He began to sob, words squeaking through the pained noises. Cursing the sky and ground, cursing everything, he wailed and still could not let go. Despite the horrible side of this wish, he was so sure that his daughter, his sweet Zoe, was not a part of it. How wrong he had been, and now look at where his greed and desire for more had gotten him. Look where it had gotten his dearest girl.

"If, beneath that golden gleam, you can still hear me, please forgive me." His tears streamed down her hardened form, and no answer came from her silent mouth. With a whimper, the king slid to the ground, still clutching the legs of Zoe.

As night fell, the king had still not left his daughters side. Seeing a cushion nearby and feeling exhausted from such a horrific day, he reached for it rest his head, but the familiar clang of metal greeted his attempt. Curling up with the hardened golden pillow, he resolved to do his best to sleep and hope that somehow sunrise would bring some renewed chance that this could all be undone. As the night passed, the soft sounds of crickets and a king sobbing at the feet of a golden statue were all that could be heard.

A ray of sunlight caused Midas to wake suddenly, his arm striking the hard metal of the pillow. Looking up after rubbing his eyes, he saw that his daughter was still frozen in a golden trance; the night had done nothing to ease this horrible curse. Though he felt like every tear he had was already shed, he began weeping anew and fell onto Zoe's feet, silently begging for his daughter to come back to him. The longer he did so, the louder his voice became. After whining and whining, he cried out the name of the deity who had granted all this to happen.

"Oh, Dionysus, in your wisdom, please help me! Your servant, Midas, chose poorly when gifted such a rich choice as you offered. I have found no joy, no peace, and no contentment; only pain and sorrow."

Tears and ragged breaths broke his voice. "If you could find the mercy to return and reverse my selfish request, I shall cease my desire for wealth. Nothing is worth more than the daughter I have lost, so take it all away if it will only bring her back to me!"

He waited and waited, but nothing transpired, not even the rustling of a breeze. It wasn't long ago that the king felt like life couldn't get any better. He was about to throw himself back onto the ground in hopeless tears when a booming voice caught him off guard.

"So, you see now the error in your choice, Midas?" standing at the entrance to the courtyard was the red-robed god, Dionysus. Beside him with a sad look on his face was the old satyr Silenus. As Midas struggled to his feet, the god continued. "You saw treasure and riches as the gateway to your happiness, but do you see how wrong this was to think?"

Midas couldn't answer and only gave a slow, sorrowful nod. Taking a hand and touching the cheek of his daughter, Midas turned back to Dionysus and pleaded.

"She is worth more than anything. Take whatever you wish, just return her back to me."

"Worth more than all the gold you have possessed?" Dionysus asked, his eyebrows raised high.

"Countless times more valuable!"

"What of the gift you received?" the god asked, his face skeptical once more. "Is she worth more than your golden touch? This power I bestowed at your request?"

The king's answer was even more certain than before.

"This is no gift, nor is it a blessing, but a curse that has stripped away every decent thing in my life!" Midas cried out. He was speaking between sobs, his eyes turning back and forth between the god and his daughter's hardened form. "Please, so I may have the chance to show her, to show Zoe, that I have learned where true worth lies. Please, allow me to live the life she wished I would, for she was always better than me. I ask for this, for another chance to get it right."

Head hanging as he continued to weep, Midas felt a touch on the top of his bowed head. When he looked up, he was no longer in the courtyard of his palace but instead on the banks of the River Pactolus with only Dionysus beside him.

"You truly wish this gift of golden touch gone, Midas?"

The king felt the heaviness in his chest and fought through the ever-building tears to answer.

"I do, but to simply wish it gone would not properly show the depths of how this has cursed me. I *beg* for it to be gone, I *plead* with you, oh Dionysus. Even if it is the last thing I shall ever have granted to me, still I need it to be taken from me."

Midas stared back at his reflection in the calm waters of the Pactolus, seeing the gray sands swirl with the changing currents. The hand of Dionysus was heavy and firm as it rested on Midas's shoulder, but as he did so, the king noticed a most peculiar thing happening in the water. Where the sand was once plain and nothing that would seem odd, now there was a glow from the bed of the river as though its golden counterpart had replaced each grain. Like flecks of treasure, the waters lit up.

Without making a sound, Dionysus lifted his hand from the king's shoulder and presented him with a small, brown branch. Midas felt a shudder as he recalled the first branch he had turned into gold and hoped that the god was not just mocking him.

The king reached forward with an unsteady hand until he felt his fingers brush the bark, but nothing of note happened next. No brilliant splash of gold, nothing magical whatsoever. Just a man holding a twig.

"It is gone!" Midas shouted, throwing the branch in celebration.

"Not gone," Dionysus said quietly. "Just...moved. Whenever you see these golden sands, you shall be reminded of this moment and what led to it wherever you may be. That is a reminder that will be most effective, wouldn't you say?"

He turned to thank Dionysus but not only had the god disappeared, but in the blink of an eye, Midas was back in his palace. Despite his return, something seemed off about his surroundings. It took a moment before he realized that it was the colors. The monochromatic gold scheme was no more! Every article his fingers had touched was as it should be, in the greens, reds, and multitude of other magnificent colors of origin.

Footsteps approached from behind him, and a voice caused his heart to swell and his eyes to fill with tears.

"Father?"

He would know the sound of his daughter's voice anywhere, and it was something he thought would never grace his ears ever again. Turning to see her trudging toward him, he knew that no amount of gold or treasure could ever be more valuable than what she meant to him.

This wisdom was the guiding light for Midas for the rest of his days, which were filled with love and joy rather than his greed for gold and riches.

Chapter Five:

The Tale of Heracles and the 12 Labors

The mighty god Zeus possessed many qualities that projected him as the powerful leader he was, but one flaw, in particular, was a consistent thorn in his side—his wandering eye. It was well known throughout Olympus and parts of the cosmos that Zeus enjoyed the company of women other than his wife, Hera. Each time he dallied, it only increased the anger and jealousy that Hera harbored deep within her heart, but one action pushed her beyond what she could handle.

For all the time Zeus spent among immortals, he chose on this day to seek out a human woman named Alcmene. She caught the thunder gods attention because her beauty was such that the god could simply not ignore it. An absolute picture of beauty. Using his magic to disguise himself as her returning husband, Alcmene took Zeus into her bed, where she became pregnant with his child. He thought himself clever and immediately departed, returning swiftly to Olympus, where he was sure his mischief would remain in secret. However, this was not the case. Hera found out that Zeus had been unfaithful yet again and his secret was no longer. The only thing protecting Alcmene was that Hera did not know with *whom* Zeus had been with.

In a rage, Hera set out to find the goddess of birth, Ilithyia. With tears in her eyes, Hera told the goddess everything she had endured at the disloyal hands of Zeus and asked what could be done to prevent any child from coming into the world due to his dalliances. After much discussion, Ilithyia arranged to sit cross-legged with her clothing knotted to avoid any children of the world from being born until Hera was sure the threat was gone.

Alcmene sensed something could be wrong with her pregnancy, but nothing seemed to stand out of the ordinary. She called her servant and midwife to her side and confessed her fears in full. Alcmene felt as though some force prevented her from giving birth and had a dream in which the goddess of childbirth was halting all children from being born. So it was that the servant, being a woman of faith and belief, set out to discover if anything was truly amiss.

The servant prayed by the temple and spoke to Ilithyia about her conversation with Hera through patience and offerings. Discovering the reason behind why Alcmene had felt as she did, the servant used deceit and trickery to convince Ilithyia that the trouble had passed. With a breath of relief, the goddess stood up and untied the knots in her clothing, releasing the ability of birth to the world once more.

By the time the servant returned to Alcmene, a child was already in her arms, napping peacefully. Tired and content, the new mother whispered the name of her child to the winds, hoping to carry it to some fortune.

"Heracles."

Hearing that Hera had sought to prevent the birth, Alcmene grew terribly worried about her son's safety. How was a mortal woman expected to stave off the attempts of a deity? Sheer might was not in her abilities, but her mind was sharp and clever, so she crafted a plan to give her son an advantage for the difficult life ahead. For all she knew, Hera would hunt Heracles for all of his days; any aid she could bring him would help her peace of mind.

The two women took Heracles to the temple and prayed aloud to Athena. Begging on their knees, they wished for the goddess to take pity on her child and take him under her protection, as he was weak and would not survive under the care of mortals. None of this was true, but they kneeled in hope that in their sporadic kindness, the gods would impart some power to the child, thus building his defenses for the bouts ahead.

Soon, hearing the prayers of the women, Athena descended to take the child in and return back to Olympus. Trusting the mother's word, Athena sought out Hera. With an open heart and gracious action, Hera took in Heracles and nursed the infant unknowing of his origin. Tasting the divine milk, Heracles suckled with such strength causing Hera significant pain. The goddess couldn't handle Heracles' unbroken thirst and pulled him away from her breast. Her milk gushed across the heavens forming the Milky Way, and with a full belly Heracles acquired the gift of the gods. Learning of Hera's pain, Athena cast the infant back to the earth where Alcmene had been patiently hoping for his return.

Joyful was that day, for not only was her son back in her arms, but he had received a great gift in his new strength. Heracles would need such things in his future; she knew this. She was unsure what the troubles would be, but in a world where Hera may seek to end him again, his power would serve him well.

Unaware that she had given aid to the very child who she had tried to prevent from existing, Hera was furious to learn of the deceit that caused Ilithyia to stand and ruin her plot. Knowing that this child of Zeus was alive, she put another plan together that she was sure would complete her intent this time. She commanded two poisonous vipers to seek out the child by the scent of Zeus and deliver their killing bite to the unsuspecting infant.

It didn't take long for the two snakes to find their prey, and with evil hisses, they slithered up to Heracles' crib. Rearing up, the two readied themselves for the strike when two small hands appeared from the crib and seized each snake below the head. The tiny hands were incredibly powerful, and within a few moments, the vipers had the life shaken from their limp forms. Heracles threw the snakes aside with an innocent laugh and continued laughing uncontrollably, causing his mother to rush in. She gave a sudden scream when she laid eyes on the two enormous serpents lifeless on the floor.

Heracles had survived the attempts on his life thus far, but the fire of revenge that Zeus had lit in Hera's heart would not soon fade.

Day by day, Heracles grew more powerful. However, it wasn't only in strength that he matured, but also in the gifts of the arts, his kind soul, and his desire to help others around him. Despite his god-like abilities, Heracles saw himself just as anyone else would—a plain, simple man who desired good wherever he went. This kind heart procured him the love of many, and soon he met and married a magnificent woman named Megara. As the years passed, she blessed him with two children; both showered with love and affection from the moment their lives began.

When a man such as Heracles exists, it is expected that he be a focal point in many conversations. As a child, it wasn't so, but with each mighty act he performed, the whispers grew into cheers, and it didn't take long for word to reach Mount Olympus. Hermes carried the news to Hera that this young man displayed unusual strength and power, knowing of her quest to abolish the child of Zeus. Thanking Hermes for his fidelity, Hera felt the flame of rage inside her light again like it had when she first learned of the boy. This time was different, though, because she wasn't aiming in the dark; she knew where he was and, more importantly, *who* he was. Her mind began spinning with all sorts of awful imaginings of what she might do to him, but then she realized how she might cause him pain of the most significant depth. In the past, she had set her sights on Heracles directly, but if she couldn't hurt a god-like man such as him, she would hurt everyone around him that he loved.

So it came to be that Heracles was outside wallowing in the sun with his wife and children, letting the warm rays sink into his skin. Suddenly the sound of rumbling filled his ears, his vision started to fade, and within moments everything went completely black.

With a violent flinch, he woke up rubbing his eyes in a sense of confusion. His head ached, and nothing at all seemed to make sense as to why any of this had occurred. Perhaps he was ill, he thought, but his whole world came crashing down when he saw the bodies of his wife and children lying unresponsive beside him. He looked down at his garments and saw blood covering his arms and torso, leading by ragged trails to each of the three kin lying in front of him. A whimpering sound came from his throat as he struggled for breath. Shaking with desperation, he clawed his way toward his family, silently pleading that this be a nightmare he would soon wake from. His fears were confirmed when his hand met the still form of his wife, and her eyes remained motionless and clouded. Reaching over and pulling the two bodies of his children close, he wept uncontrollably as he held his family to his chest. Inhuman sounds echoed across the fields, each one more pained than the last.

Heracles stayed unmoving for longer than he knew; the sun rose and set before he even contemplated anything at all. He couldn't seem to piece together what had happened, and no amount of searching in his mind would bring fourth an answer. He craved for answers. Or if there were no answers to be had, perhaps he could seek absolution for this horrible deed he had committed. Whether he remembered it or not was not his focus; the fact remained that when he thought back, one moment they were alive and the next revealed the bloody scene he had woken to.

In all the land, he knew of one being who could bring him what he desired, either answers or salvation for his tortured soul: the Oracle of Delphi. He was determined to find some way to absolve himself of these horrors. No sacrifice would be too great a price to pay for whatever had transpired in the time he didn't remember. Whatever had happened, he held himself responsible.

While it was true that the Oracle held the power to grant such things to Heracles, Hera was one step ahead of him. Hearing his cries to the heavens, she visited the Oracle and, through her cunning and influential nature, convinced the Oracle to ignore the pleading of Heracles causing him even further torment.

Heracles finally arrived at Temple of Apollo and met the Oracle in a state of humility, bowed and sorrowful. He begged for any answer to his plight, any possibility that he could cleanse himself of the disastrous incident he awoke to. In any other circumstance, the Oracle would have used her wisdom to peer into the darkness and aid the weary, but Hera was mighty and terrible when crossed. So the Oracle heeded the goddess instead.

"There is but one way that you can begin to heal for the horrors you have caused," the Oracle whispered, her voice enchanting, capturing his undivided attention. "Take yourself to the kingdom ruled by Eurystheus. Do what he asks of you, and do so without fail."

"How long shall my servitude to the king last, oh Oracle?" the kneeling Heracles questioned.

"You will know when it is time Heracles, and only then shall you have redeemed yourself."

The Oracle turned away, leaving Heracles to ponder over what he had just heard. What would this king demand of him? Would he be capable of such a task? How would he know when his time was up? Countless questions sparked within the mind of Heracles. However, his newfound quest remained at the forefront, and so he set off for the distant kingdom that awaited him.

There have been many kings worthy of their title who provided times of prosperity and pride to their land; Eurystheus was not one of those men. When necessity and ill-timing collide, they produce the kind of ruler that Eurystheus embodied; unsure and self-righteous for no earned reason. A weak lineage sent his father to an early grave, leaving an immature child to ascend the throne. The royal court experienced the full brunt of his irrational anger and his incompetence to rule, which more often than not, ended in some form of carnage. It was into this that Heracles took himself willingly.

The king was even more insufferable than Heracles had expected, worsened still by the kings eerie seers. The seers had foretold of a great hero's arrival, and that despite his power and strength, he would offer his service. And so, Heracles acknowledged the truth in their visions and bowed his knee to Eurystheus, vowing to serve him as the Oracle had instructed.

"If you are to be in my service, then you will do as I command!" shouted the king in a nasal, whining voice. He was immature in every action and took far too much glee in the prospect of unleashing Heracles onto his enemies. Eurystheus thought for a while about where Heracles would be best suited to being his labors when he clapped his hands together and shouted three words to the court.

"The Nemean Lion!"

This brought a barrage of whispers and concerned tones from all those present, causing Heracles to question what he was tasked to do. A lion didn't seem as if it would pose much of a threat to the mighty Heracles, but it was not a beast to underestimate, as the king went on to explain. Not a single man had been able to subdue this vicious beast, and anyone that crossed its path would encounter their demise.

"I expect for you to die out there Heracles, but if not, then an awful beast has been removed from these lands." the king said. "Though I doubt you shall return, bring me back a trophy of this lion to prove your worth." and just like that, he sent Heracles away to seek out the Nemean Lion.

The town of Cleonae was the last known location of the lion, and so that is where Heracles set off. Unsure of exactly what he was going to be facing, Heracles prepared several arrows so that he could react at a moment's notice. Unfortunately, the king had not informed Heracles of the lion's impenetrable fur, thus setting him up for further failure. Heracles soon discovered this bewildering feature as the lion prowled into view and an arrow, fired straight and true, ricocheted harmlessly to the side, alerting the massive beast of his presence.

After loosing the remaining arrows with the same ineffective result, Heracles led the beast on a winding chase back to its cavernous dwelling. In an enormous tussle, and in a moment of opportunity, Heracles stunned the roaring beast with a swift blow to its gigantic skull. With little desire to waste any more time, Heracles mustered all of his strength, and squeezed until he felt the life leaving the beast's body. With a final gasp, the lion slumped, dead.

Knowing that the tale alone would not be sufficient enough to verify his triumph over the Nemean Lion, Heracles took his blade out in an effort to remove the hide, but it was to no avail. The sharp blade could not pierce through the lions tough skin, but then a clever idea struck Heracles! Using the lion's own claws, he skinned the hide from the lifeless beast and began to make his triumphant return back to weakling king, Eurystheus.

Thirty days had passed since Heracles set out on his perilous quest. Eurystheus was sitting in his throne room when a servant scurried in with word that Heracles had survived and quickly approached the kingdom. With a wheeze, the king leapt to his feet and hurried to the stronghold's main gates. There stood Heracles, draped in the pelt of the notorious Nemean Lion, waiting below him.

"Halt!" Eurystheus roared, his guards readying a barrage of arrows toward Heracles from high above the palace walls. "It is apparent to me that though you have returned, it would be hazardous to welcome you within the walls of my kingdom. You have proved yourself to be quite the dangerous man. You may decide to turn on me or my people without warning, which I cannot allow. So from this day forward, you shall come *only* to the gates of my fortress, and no longer may you enter inside. You shall receive instruction from my messenger, *and no longer from me*. And, Heracles," he added with a cruel sneer, "don't expect these tasks to become any easier! Now, wait for word of your next quest!"

In a flourish, the king left Heracles standing at the gates.

Eurystheus spoke the truth, for the next day, it was a messenger who arrived in the morning with news of Heracles' next labor. A colossal, two-headed hydra that Hera herself had conjured was residing in a large murky lake outside of a nearby town. No one could get near it for fear of the poisonous fumes that lingered about the monster's lair. Heracles was commanded to slay the serpentine water monster and return back to the gates from which he currently stood.

Upon arriving at the outskirts of the lair, Heracles concealed himself behind some rocky terrain patiently waiting to see if the hydra would make itself known on its own accord. After some time, he determined that the monster might not emerge from its burrow unless provoked, but Heracles didn't want to get close enough for the serpent to take him by surprise. Notching an arrow, he leaned back and let it fly right into the nest of the beast, where something deep inside met it with a thunderous growl. With more hustle than ever expected, the hydra lurched out into the daylight, both its heads snapping and hissing, craving to learn what had disturbed its slumber.

Knowing that he had to be swift, Heracles sped out from his hiding place and lunged at one of the beast's head with his sword. Employing the element of surprise, the head tumbled from the now-flailing neck of the serpent, and the remaining head gave a pained bark. Heracles figured that this would be a much easier kill than expected, but then a wet, squelching sound came from the neck of the hydra. And from the bloody stump grew two new heads, each as vicious as the first.

His eyes widened as he watched this rebirth happen right in front of him, but there was no time to be standing in disbelief. Instead, he tightly gripped his blade and hacked away once more; one head fell, but two more appeared. No matter the speed of his strike, or how hard he swung, the severed heads gave way for two new ones until there were over a dozen; all glaring deep into his soul, ready to strike.

There had to be some way to prevent this cycle of regeneration, but nothing seemed to come to mind. Heracles noticed that each time a head was severed from the neck, the stump would ooze a thick, steaming liquid that sizzled when it hit the ground. This gave him an idea. In a flash of genius, he reached for his torch with his off hand, and before a new head began its regenerative process, he plunged the torch deep into the bleeding neck. Heracles discovered that the stump was no longer raw; instead, it was charred black and firm as the flame had cauterized the wound. Several seconds passed, but no heads sprung forth from each blackened neck. Finally, after what felt like an eternity, Heracles stood breathless in the middle of a bloody scene indeed. Heads were all about the place, and in the middle of it all was the lifeless form of the venomous hydra. Heracles wiped his sword clean and with a deep sigh he prepared for his journey back toward the kingdom, where yet another task surely awaited.

Each time Heracles completed a task and returned safely to the palace, Eurystheus would grow more and more enraged. Hera even began revealing horrific and monstrous visions within the kings dreams in hopes to muster even more difficult tasks for Heracles to undertake, but his might was drastically underestimated.

After the hydra's downfall, Eurystheus ordered his messenger to send Heracles off to capture the ever-elusive Ceryneian Hind; a small deer that was faster and more agile than any man could ever hope to be. The king hoped that despite Heracles' impressive strength, his ability to chase and outlast the Hind would surely fail.

Yet again, though, the king did not extend any commendations toward Heracles as he waved him off. Instead, he snickered and fantasized about all of the possibilities of his demise, fully expecting to never see him again. Heracles did indeed have more trouble than he had first anticipated, but his resilience and dedication never wavered once. For over a year, the Hind evaded his clutches, but every time he fell short, it only hardened his resolve. When he finally did manage to catch the elusive deer, coercing it to trip on a trap he had set, his quest was seemingly not over. Just as Heracles was binding the majestic creature in preparation for the journey back to Eurystheus, Artemis, goddess of the hunt, appeared before him in a rage. Heracles was sure that this would be his end until he was demanded to explain, in depth, of his reasoning for capturing her prized Hind.

Artemis had heard rumors of Hera's hatred toward Heracles and how she was puppeteering Eurystheus to bring further torment to Heracles through many grueling labors. Usually, she would not have considered mercy, but the truth was in his eyes as well as his story, so she decided to let him depart unharmed *and* with her beloved Hind as well. Heracles made a solemn vow to Artemis that once he had completed this third labor, the Hind would be released and freed to live out its life, unscathed.

His word remained true, for once Eurystheus laid eyes on the majestic deer, Heracles set the Hind loose and watched on as it sped off to freedom. This only added fuel to the anger growing inside of King Eurystheus, as every time Heracles was sent off on an impossible task, he would return triumphant procuring more and more glory for his efforts.

Infuriated, the king sent Heracles off on yet another quest to capture the hulking Erymanthian Boar for the fourth of his tasks, but he wanted to add something of an added challenge. Instead of simply slaying the beast and returning with its pelt, this time, Heracles was ordered to carry the boar back alive. Eurystheus was certain that he had devised a quest that would be so difficult, it would be sure to spell doom for our dear Heracles.

On his way to Mount Erymanthos, Heracles sought information from whoever he could find about this boar and how he may go about catching it, but the only answer he ever heard back in response was that a centaur named Chiron was the only one they knew to have ever captured the beast. It took Heracles many months to finally reach the centaur's dwelling, and by the time he did, the snow was thick and tough to maneuver. As fate would have it, the snow was precisely what Heracles would need, according to Chiron. The old, yet wise centaur presented Heracles with the secret knowledge that if he coerced the boar into the snow, it would slow the beast just enough to capture it without causing any harm. Heracles did just that, and the moment the boar charged into the snow, Heracles covered the beast with a heavy net. The panicked hog cried and squealed as it realized its mistake. It was only a matter of tying up the beast before carrying it back to the kingdom. Once

Eurystheus caught sight of the massive boar, still kicking against Heracles' grip, he frantically cried out to all those within ears reach.

"Away with it! Don't let him bring that ghastly beast any closer!"

The messenger hurried out to stop Heracles far from the palace gates as per the kings request. Heracles cut the bonds on the boar with a wry smile, and it hurried off into the distance almost snorting with glee. Only then did the messenger explain what task awaited him next, which Eurystheus was confident would finally cause Heracles to stumble and fail.

Several leagues away resided the province of King Augeas, who kept a stable filled with immortal cattle. As the messenger told Heracles, the stables had not been scrubbed for 30 years, and the number of livestock had grown to a whopping 1,000 within the herd. Not only was the work deemed impossible, but the humiliation suffered by failing would also bring Heracles the shame that both Hera and Eurystheus were yearning for.

However, Heracles did not think like any other. Instead, he set off for where the rivers Alpheus and Peneus met, adjacent to the stables. Digging deep trenches, he redirected the canals to gush directly into the stables, blasting away the decades of filth that had built up. The stout cattle stood safely as the water rushed around them, proving yet again that Heracles had found victory where others could not.

By this time, you would think that there would be some hint of doubt in the mind of Eurystheus, but his resolve was all the more absolute. Upon hearing how Heracles had once again prospered, he decided that the rivers' might and not Heracles' strength won the day, so the king would not recognize this triumph.

"Tell Heracles that I shall not consider this task complete, and that he must attend to another," the king shouted to the messenger, desperate to grasp some form of control in the whole matter.

The next task that Heracles was given would prove to be his most challenging, and exposed to the world how the gods played sides in the lives of men. The king demanded that Heracles drive off the Stymphalian Birds; man-eating creatures with bronze beaks and razor-sharp feathers that could slice through their prey. The flock had migrated to a lake in Arcadia, where they took over the countryside, dropping toxic dung and poisoning the entire water supply for nearby regions. The people grew tired of waking to their crops and fruit plantations ravaged from the birds, and if they tried to defend their harvests they would pay the ultimate price.

When Heracles arrived, he could not get close to the birds due to the horrible fumes and toxicity surrounding the lake. No amount of profound movement or shouts seemed to affect the birds in the slightest. The goddess Athena appeared seeing that Heracles was in a state of indecision and gifted Heracles with a helpful tool that Hephaestus had crafted to aid in this task. Hera was influencing the king, and so the gods considered there must be fair play on all sides. Athena handed Heracles an ornate rattle that would drive the birds into the air. The tool from the gods worked precisely as intended, and once the birds were in the air, Heracles drew back his bowstring and continued to strike each one down with penetrating arrows. After losing many of their flock, the rest of the birds flew away, leaving the lake and the land of Arcadia free of any more torment.

Once again, furious that yet another task had failed to overcome Heracles, Eurystheus wasted no time in commanding him to capture the feared Cretan Bull. Many had tried to calm the beast, but the swift horns and brute strength always got the better of those bold enough to attempt such a feat. Heracles, however, knew better and kept his distance while he waited for the bull to succumb to fatigue. Hours passed before the bull finally began to tire, and only then did Heracles make his move.

Leaping out of the way of the bulls final charge, Heracles latched his arms around the bull's neck and held tight. The animal lurched and lunged all about, trying to throw Heracles from its neck, but it was to no avail. Slowly the bull gave in, and the beast collapsed down to the ground as it accepted its defeat. After carefully tying the bull up, Heracles set off on the return journey, leaving the shores of Crete behind him.

With the delivery of the Cretan Bull at the gates, Eurystheus called for the beast to be sacrificed immediately as an offering to Hera. The offering, however, was rejected by the goddess because it reflected the glory of her adversary, Heracles. Unfortunately, for the people of Greece, the bull was later released by the king, causing unforgivable havoc to all those in its path.

The eighth labor arranged for Heracles was to navigate to the lands of Thrace and fetch four blood-thirsty mares from the barbaric king of the Bistones, King Diomedes. Each of the crazed mares Podargos, Lampon, Xanthos, and Deinos were all kept tethered with iron chains due to their aggressive nature. The madness of the mares formulated from their desire for human flesh, frequently torn from the bodies of unsuspecting visitors or captives the barbaric king deemed worthy to sacrifice. After hearing of this trial, Heracles concluded that help would be needed to avoid unnecessary harm while rounding up these mares. Despite asking countless individuals, only a small cohort of volunteers agreed to join his crew; one of which was a young fellow named Abderus.

Heracles and his new companions got along quite well, and the journey didn't seem as long with fresh faces to share tales and conversation with. A plan was devised between the crew to sneak in and shatter the chains that detained the mares. Next, they would direct the mares toward the coastline where their ship would be docked in wait of their arrival. Everything was going to plan; Heracles quickly disposed of the guards on watch, and entered the stable to find the four mares within. However, the moment Heracles rattled the chains to break them free, the horses went into a frenzy of neighs, surely alerting everyone within ears reach.

Quickly rounding the four mares together, Heracles and Abderus hurried down to the water's edge. Heracles was just about to load the horses onto the ship when Abderus shouted and pointed to the higher ground from where they had just left. Turning, Heracles saw the barbaric leader, Diomedes, eyes flaming with rage.

Heracles handed the reins to Abderus and instructed him to care for the mares while he handled Diomedes and his band of savages. It didn't take him long to subdue the king, but when he returned with the unconscious Diomedes, Heracles found to his horror that the mares had devoured Abderus. In a burst of anger, Heracles dumped Diomedes and watched as the mares set upon him. Calmed from their recent feast, Heracles used this opportunity to tie-up the mares and set sail for the kingdom, and yet another challenge.

In an effort to please the gods, Eurystheus ordered that the four horses be presented to Zeus as a sacrifice. Although, just like Hera, Zeus refused to accept the proposal, leading the mares off to run free despite the king's pleas.

Before the king could send the message of another quest to Heracles, Eurystheus' daughter came to him and demanded of a gift. Of all the things she could have asked for, the princess had heard tell of a magnificent girdle belonging to Hippolyta, queen of the Amazons. It had been a gift to the queen from her father, Ares, but the princess of Tiryns now desired to have it for herself. Just as her father, Eurystheus, was selfish and blinded by greed, so was the princess filled with the same afflictions. Not ever wanting to deny his daughter anything, the king ordered that Heracles leave immediately and only return with Hippolyta's belt in his possession.

For years Heracles had toiled under the stress of these never-ending quests, but now he had gained a crew to help bear the weight of this burden. The road to finding the belt was not only treacherous, but not many knew the exact path that one must take. And so Heracles and his band of men set sail until they reached the island of Paros. Living on this island were the sons of Minos; the king of Crete and son of Zeus. Unaccustomed to having outsiders walk on their shores, the sons immediately felt threatened.

It wasn't long after the group had landed on the island that the sons captured and killed two of Heracles' men, demanding that they depart and never return lest the rest of them meet the same end. This sent waves of anger through Heracles, and in a bloody rage, he set upon the sons killing two of them to match the murders they had committed.

"An eye for an eye," Heracles yelled into the forest, "unless you send two men to take the places of those you killed, the rest of you will meet the fate that your brothers did!"

The sons of Minos did not doubt the word of Heracles after seeing how swiftly he had killed their two brothers, so they sent out two men that joined Heracles on his quest. Moving quickly, they sailed off to seek the belt of Hippolyta once more.

They docked next in a land ruled by the court of Lycus. Seeing the hero and his men sailing up to their coast, Lycus begged Heracles to support them in battle. For years, King Mygdon had been at war with Lycus and his people, but there was no victory in sight. Feeling pity in his heart for this man, Heracles agreed to lend his blade and that of his men. After weeks of combat, Lycus and Heracles emerged victorious over King Mygdon. As Lycus looked over his vast new kingdom, he desired to honor Heracles and did so by naming all the new land he had acquired *Heraclea* after the hero who had helped him obtain it.

It was with the blessings of Lycus that Hippolyta heard of the victories that Heracles had won, and she was so impressed that she presented the belt to him as an offering upon his arrival at Themiscyra.

In the middle of that very night, Hera took it upon herself to try and stop yet another triumph of Heracles from coming to pass. Disguised as one of Hippolyta's women, Hera creeped throughout the camp spreading horrible rumors of Heracles and his men. By the time morning came, the entire camp was up in arms, ready to ride in and destroy them.

Heracles was conversing with his men when off in the distance he saw Hippolyta and her tribeswomen racing over the horizon, weapons drawn and eyes ablaze. He had found treachery from the gods before, and so he readied the men into a defensive formation. The warriors of Hippolyta were no match for Heracles, and they were swiftly cut down, with the girdle seized and the day seemingly won. No one but Hera knew that the carnage could have been avoided, and so Heracles set sail for Eurystheus's kingdom once more, wondering if this ordeal would ever end.

When Heracles returned with the girdle, Eurystheus' messenger was ready with yet another labor for the mighty Heracles. In the far west, on the island of Erytheia, lived a giant named Geryon, famed for his precious cattle. So closely guarded was this herd of cattle that it was said that no one had ever been able to lure a single cow away.

The road to Geryon was long and forced Heracles to make his way across the sweltering Libyan desert. So hot were the days and so lonely was his journey that he raged against the very sun that beat down on him. Pulling an arrow from his quiver, he fired a shot directly into the sun. Just as he was about to continue, the sun-god, Helios, appeared before him in the sand holding the very arrow that Heracles had just fired.

"Quite a show of bravery to fire at the sun-god, you know," said Helios, handing the arrow back to Heracles. "I haven't met anyone else with such courage, so I present to you a gift."

Helios gifted Heracles a bronze cup used to sail the skies from east to west every day. Swift and sure in its speed, the offering was a treasure indeed. Using his new prize, Heracles made great haste and reached his next destination in no time, the land of Erytheia. It wasn't soon after he made landfall that he heard an awful roar and turned to see a massive two-headed dog dashing toward him. Orthrus the two-headed dog, belonged to the mythical herdsman, Eurytion. Both in charge of guarding Geryon's prized cattle.

Lifting his mighty club, Heracles slew the powerful dog with a single blow, though the noise alerted Eurytion, who was nearby attending to his herd. Try as he might, the herdsman was no match for Heracles either and quickly met the same fate as the menacing two-headed canine.

The cries from both Orthrus and Eurytion caused the monstrous Geryon to wake from his slumber. Armed with a shield, lances, and a bronze helmet, the monster set out to find the source of all the commotion. Heracles and Geryon pursued each other and fought tirelessly until, on the banks of the river Anthemus, Heracles let an arrow fly that drove straight through the helmet and into the forehead of the monster. Bellowing an awful scream, blood pouring from his face, Geryon fell to the ground, dead.

Rallying the cattle together, Heracles believed that he had accomplished yet another task and was ready to return to the kingdom where Eurystheus would be waiting with another seemingly impossible labor. Hera, however, had different plans, and so she conjured a swarm of flies to irritate the cattle until they scattered across the land. Not to be deterred, Heracles spent the next year scurrying to gather every last one of the cattle. When he finally had the herd back together, Hera sent a flood to raise the water level of the river to halt their progress. Not one to be bested, Heracles piled stone after stone into the river, raising the riverbed and allowing the cattle to safely cross.

After the long journey, Heracles finally arrived back at the palace gates with the cattle, much to the surprise of Eurystheus' entire court. Immediately seizing the herd, the king sacrificed them to appease Hera. Still, as before, she turned away at the sight of the offering, not wanting to give Heracles any glory whatsoever.

Heracles demanded to see Eurystheus, claiming that his servitude was complete and the labors promised had been done. The king was not satisfied, though, and responded with a firm denial.

"You did not accomplish all of these tasks on your own, which was what your labors demanded of you. Because of this, you still have two more labors before you are free of your oath to me," Eurystheus said, laughing all the while.

These words sent anger throughout Heracles' body, but he knew that until Eurystheus released him, there was nothing he could do. With a bowed head and humbled spirit, he readied himself for the next labor.

The first of the two final labors was for Heracles to steal three golden apples from the orchard belonging to the Hesperides, the nymphs of golden sunsets and evening light. The first objective for Heracles was find where this orchard was concealed. From rumor, he heard that there was an old shape-shifting sea god who could give him this information, so he set out to find him. It was a short mission that ended up with Heracles catching the elusive god disguised as an older man. Not wanting to be harmed, the sea god gave Heracles what he was asking for with haste.

Following the instructions given to him by the sea god, Heracles found his way to the entrance to the Hesperides' garden, where even the air seemed to be filled with life. Everything was vibrant, and a light morning dew dampened the grass. He began looking around when a voice startled him so much that he nearly fell over as he spun around to face it.

"What business have you here?" demanded the figure before Heracles. It was Atlas, the Titan cursed to hold the weight of the world on his shoulders.

"I have come to do the bidding of King Eurystheus, which is for me to return with three golden apples from this very orchard," Heracles responded, looking in awe at the massive globe on the shoulders of Atlas.

"That is surely impossible, for you will not be able to get close enough to even smell them."

"Why is this?" Heracles questioned.

"Only those who are related to the proprietor of this garden can move freely amongst the trees and are welcome to its fruits."

"And where would I find a relative of the Hesperides to fetch the fruit for me?" Heracles asked, growing irritated at the prospect of not being able to follow through after being in servitude for so long.

"You are fortunate, for in my veins runs the same blood like that of the Hesperides. I only ask that you hold this weight for me, as the curse cannot end. I shall go and retrieve the apples you so desire and return to take back my burden."

This plan sounded perfect to Heracles, and a short while of holding the globe seemed worthy of the result. Atlas carefully rested the globe onto Heracles' shoulders and set off deep into the garden. Within an hour, he returned with the three golden apples, and just before he reached for the globe, Atlas took a step back. Heracles raised an eyebrow and, shifting the massive weight on his back, questioned Atlas in earnest.

"What is this? Are you backing out of our deal?" he asked, his voice filled with worry.

"I have no desire to be back under that weight and curse, so why shouldn't I depart now and be free of it forever?"

Heracles knew he had to think quickly, so he devised a plan to trick the Titan.

"Oh, Atlas, you have gotten the best of me, truly you have," Heracles said humbly. "If only you will give me a moment free from the weight to shift my robe, I will take the curse forever."

Atlas, not thinking clearly considering how close he was to freedom, agreed and took the globe, expecting Heracles to adjust his clothing and take it back. However, Heracles picked up the golden apples and ran off without a word, leaving Atlas back where he started, cursed and hobbled by the weight of the world.

When Heracles returned to the palace gates, he heard the raging of Eurystheus inside, so great was his anger. He was absolutely sure that *this* would be the labor that finally ended Heracles, but instead, here he was, one task away from his freedom. In some deep part of himself, the king was tired of this whole ordeal. In the beginning, he had been impassioned and inspired to create difficulty and trust his visions, but now it had been years and years, each more disappointing than the one before. No matter the challenge or task, Heracles overcame it and returned with more glory than ever before. There was one last chance to stand triumphant for both the king and Hera, but if this did not succeed, he saw himself giving in to the exhaustion growing within him.

If there was one single place that would be absolute in its treatment of Heracles, it was the Underworld. Thus far, every test took Heracles to the ends of the earth, but now was the time for him to be sent into the depths where only the dead dare to dwell. As if that wasn't enough, the task was not to simply enter the Underworld; it was to capture the guardian of the gates itself, Cerberus, the three-headed hound with the tail of a dragon. The very thought sent fear deep into the heart of Heracles, but he knew that if he survived, then this entire ordeal would come to an end.

The realm of the dead didn't accept just anyone, and for this particular feat, Heracles would need to seek assistance beyond the realm of man. The Eleusinian Mysteries were the most secret of religious groups and held the secrets of the ages. After traveling to Athens, he was successfully initiated into the Mysteries and was granted access to the Underworld, but he still needed more help. The gods knew that this labor was the most important of all and began to offer their support to the hero.

With the protection and guidance of the two deities; Hermes and Athena, Heracles made his way to the depths of the Underworld. However, on their way, the group encountered two of Hades' prisoners, Theseus and Pirithous. These two men were detained for their attempt to capture the queen of the Underworld, Persephone. Exposing their scheme, Hades had forced the men into bindings and an eternity of torment. They begged Heracles to free them, for years had passed since their imprisonment. Heracles stepped toward Theseus, now full of remorse was freed from his bindings. However, when Heracles tried to free Pirithous, the prisoner still had his heart and mind set on Persephone, so the binds would not budge. Realizing his fate, the man wept horribly as the group were left with no choice but to depart without him, leaving Pirithous to his eternal doom.

After searching for quite some time, Heracles stumbled into a colossal chamber and into the presence of Hades himself. Heracles had been through so much, so there was no room for fear in his heart. With nothing but the burning desire to be free, he marched forward and spoke directly to the ruler of the Underworld.

"Hades," he began, his voice absolute and sure, "I am here to complete a task that shall lead to my freedom, and all that stands in my way is your consent."

"Consent for what, mortal?" asked Hades, glaring down at him from his dark throne.

"Permission to take Cerberus, your guardian of the gates, back to the kingdom of Eurystheus. Only then will I be freed from my servitude, and once I am a free man, I shall lead the guardian back to the gates he is sworn to protect."

Hades appeared unsure, though he had heard many tales of Heracles glorious accomplishments.

After taking some time to consider, the god answered.

"If you can, without a single weapon, subdue the beast, then you have my permission to take Cerberus with you. If you fail this task, you shall not receive my protection as he tears you to shreds."

Heracles agreed to this immediately and set off toward the gates. Cerberus was more than Heracles had expected, each head dripping drool from between its sharpened fangs. Its body gleamed from the hellish flames all about, and with a few quick sniffs Cerberus began barking in a deep, demonic tone when Heracles approached. In a surprisingly speedy ordeal, Heracles dove beneath the dog and, with his bare hands, wrestled the beast into an unconscious state. Heracles slung the dog onto his back despite the considerable weight and began to make his way up out of the infernal depths of the Underworld.

"My lord, it would be best if you came to see this yourself," said the servant of Eurystheus, eyes fearful and voice stammering. The king argued but eventually agreed to follow the frightened servant all the way to the palace gates. Without a word, the servant pointed down, and Eurystheus suddenly gasped as he saw Heracles standing next to the sleeping form of Cerberus. It was surely impossible, the king thought, for no one could journey into the Underworld and return, let alone bring back the guardian of the gates with him.

"Take that beast away from here!" bellowed the king. "Go free, never return, it is yours to take; just get that hellish beast away from my kingdom. NOW!"

Heracles held the king to his words, and once Eurystheus granted his freedom, the hero took the still-unconscious canine back to Hades. It had been too long since he had taken a genuinely free breath, and it tasted just as sweet as he remembered.

After years of toil, Heracles had finally redeemed the tragic deaths of his family and earned a place in the divine pantheon. But his triumphs held an even deeper significance. In overcoming the chaotic and evil forces of the world, the hero swept away what remained of the Titans' primordial order, reshaping it into one where humanity could thrive. Through his labors, Heracles tamed the world's madness by atoning for his own.

CONCLUSION

You have ascended to the top of Mount Olympus and fraternized with the gods. You've explored strange places with fantastic creatures and folk. With new eyes, you have been taken to a world that you knew but now understand more profoundly.

Greek mythology is a beautiful mixture of culture and worship with just the right touch of humanity, and it is the purpose of this book to show you all of that.

May this start be the catalyst that brings you back time and time again and sends you to discover fresh, untouched realms. You can find inspiration in almost everything, and for the time within these pages, perhaps you found yours in the brilliant lives of these characters.

Never stop learning and growing, for if the Greeks taught us anything, it is that life can be wild and chaotic, but it is also precious.

The world is big, but the world of mythology is bigger.

Happy exploring!

www.ingramcontent.com/pod-product-compliance
Lightning Source LLC
Chambersburg PA
CBHW070104120526
44588CB00034B/2251